THE LANGUAGE OF FLOWERS

AN ANTHOLOGY OF POETRY AND PROSE

LORENZ BOOKS

NEW YORK • LONDON • SYDNEY • BATH

This edition published in the UK by Lorenz Books

This edition published in the USA by Lorenz Books
27 West 20th Street, New York, NY 10011.

Lorenz Books are available for bulk purchase for sales promotion and for
premium use. For details write or call the manager of special sales:
Lorenz Books, 27 West 20th Street, New York, NY 10011.

© Anness Publishing Limited 1997

Lorenz Books is an imprint of
Anness Publishing Limited

ISBN 1 85967 334 1

Printed in China

1 3 5 7 9 10 8 6 4 2

CONTENTS

INTRODUCTION

From the delicacy of the wild primrose to the splendour of the hothouse orchid, flowers have been a favourite subject of writers throughout the ages. Poets and botanists, novelists and gardeners have all sought to celebrate them. Sometimes they inspire honour, sometimes sadness, but always an appreciation of their wonderful variety and of the scents, shapes and colours that distinguish them.

As well as being loved for their beauty and fragrance, however, flowers have also come to symbolize specific ideas and to be associated with certain moods. The last rose of summer marks the passing of the old year, while the snowdrop is widely recognized as the herald of spring and of new life.

Over the centuries a whole language of flowers was gradually developed, particularly by lovers who wished to send secret messages to each other; a carefully chosen bouquet could be as eloquent as a written letter. To send clematis with white lilies and ivy, for example, would signify "I admire your intelligence and respect you. Will you marry me?"; to which the reply might come in the form of a disdainful sunflower, too grand to accept, or a more encouraging posy of blue periwinkles offering friendship.

Anyone wishing to revive this delightful practice is sure to find here a flower to convey their feelings. With a wide-ranging selection from among the best-known plants, both wild and cultivated, the following pages form an enchanting garden full of hidden meaning.

ALCEA

HOLLYHOCK

Ambition, Fecundity

I am no Florist, at least not a Scientific one, but I have enough independence of mind to judge for myself without asking the self-named Connoisseurs when I must be pleased and when I must criticize what they are pleased to denounce as the inferior works of Nature. All have their characteristic beauties & in my parterre the humble Cowslip, or the unpretending Foxglove finds as hearty a welcome as the Crown Imperial or the stately and exuberant Holyoake.

FROM *MY HOUSE AND GARDEN* (1828) BY

JAMES LUCKOCK

ANEMONE
WINDFLOWER

Forsaken

The wood-anemonie through dead oak-leaves
And in the thickest wood now blooms anew
And where the green briar and the bramble weaves
Thick clumps o' green anemonies thicker grew
And weeping flowers in thousands pearled in dew
People the woods and brake's hid hollows there
White, yellow, and purple-hued the wide wood through
What pretty drooping weeping flowers they are.
The clipt frilled leaves the slender stalk they bear
On which the drooping flower hangs, weeping dew.

FROM *WOOD-ANEMONIE* BY JOHN CLARE (1793–1864)

ANTIRRHINUM

SNAPDRAGON

Presumption

Oh, how useful and beautiful are the tall yellow and the tall white Snapdragons! They can be played with in so many ways: potted up in the autumn, grown and flowered in a green house, cut back and planted out in the spring to flower again, admirable to send away; in fact, they have endless merits, and in a large clump in front of some dark corner or shrub they look very handsome indeed. They are lovely picked and on the dinner-table, especially the yellow Snapdragons, but, like many other things, they just want a little care and cultivation, which they often do not get; and they ought to be sown every April, and again in July.

FROM *POT-POURRI FROM A SURREY GARDEN* BY MRS C.W. EARLE

(1836–1925)

AQUILEGIA
COLUMBINE

Folly

Still, still my eye will gaze long fixed on thee.
Till I forget that I am called a man,
And at thy side fast-rooted seem to be,
And the breeze comes my cheek with thine to fan.
Upon this craggy hill our life shall pass,
A life of summer days and summer joys,
Nodding our honey-bells mid pliant grass
In which the bee half-hid his time employs…

FROM *THE COLUMBINE* BY JONES VERY (1813–80)

ASTER
MICHAELMAS DAISY

Afterthought

The Michaelmas Daisies, among dede weedes,
Bloom for St. Michael's valorous deedes,
And seem the last of the flowers that stoode
Till the feast of St. Simon and St. Jude.

ANON, FROM AN EARLY CALENDAR OF ENGLISH FLOWERS

BELLIS PERENNIS
ENGLISH DAISY

Innocence

D idn't you know that?' cried another Daisy, and here they all began shouting together, till the air seemed quite full of little shrill voices. "Silence, every one of you!" cried the Tiger-lily, waving itself passionately from side to side and trembling with excitement. "They know I can't get at them!" it panted, bending its quivering head towards Alice, "or they wouldn't dare to do it!"

"Never mind," Alice said in a soothing tone, and stooping down to the daisies, who were beginning again, she whispered, "If you don't hold your tongues, I'll pick you!"

There was silence in a moment, and several of the pink daisies turned white. "That's right!" said the Tiger-lily. "The daisies are worst of all. When one speaks, they all begin together, and it's enough to make one wither to hear the way they go on!"

FROM *THROUGH THE LOOKING GLASS* BY LEWIS CARROLL (1832-98)

CAMPANULA

BELLFLOWER

———

Constancy

Great clusters of campanulas hang from all the ledges, giving to the rocks a peculiarly home-like appearance...though closely resembling the slender bluebell, that springs elastic from the airy tread of the Scottish maiden on the Highland bank, it is not the same. It has more luxuriant foliage, its colour is of a deeper and more purplish blue, and its corolla is wider in the mouth and flatter in the shape – a peculiarity which belongs to all the Italian campanulas, and distinguishes them from all others – while its roots are larger and thicker. Still, in spite of these differences, it is so like our own familiar flower, that it awoke a thrill of pleasant recognition in my heart, and gathered to itself a host of tender memories of far-off scenes.

FROM *THE RIVIERA* BY HUGH MACMILLAN (1833-1903)

Cheiranthus
WALLFLOWER

Fidelity in adversity

Flower in the crannied wall,
I pluck you out of the crannies;
Hold you here, root and all, in my hand,
Little flower — but if I could understand
What you are, root and all, and all in all,
I should know what God and man is.

ALFRED, LORD TENNYSON (1809-92)

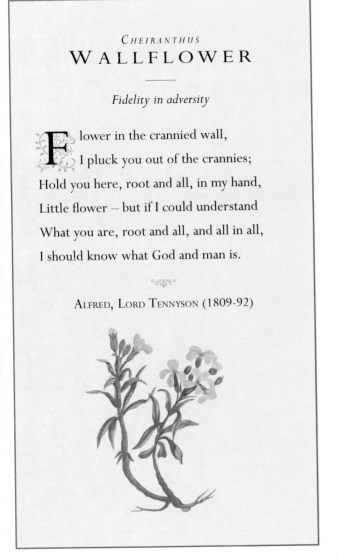

CHRYSANTHEMUM

White: Truth, Red: I love, Yellow: Slighted love

Oh, that you could see my chrysanthemums. I have one out now unlike any I ever saw. It is the shape and size of a large honeysuckle, and the inside filled up with tubes. Each of the petals or florets (which are they?) is, on the outside, of a deep violet colour, getting, however, paler as it approaches the end, and the inside shows itself much like the inside of a honeysuckle tube, of a shining silver white, just, in some particular lights, tinged with purple. I never saw so elegant a flower of any sort; and my jar of four kinds, golden, lemon, yellow, purple, lilac, crimson and pink, exceeds in brilliancy any display that I ever witnessed.

MARY RUSSELL MITFORD (1787-1855) TO EMILY JEPHSON,
DECEMBER 1830

CISTUS

ROCK ROSE

Popular favour

A better claim Sweet Cistus may pretend,
    Whose sweating leaves a fragrant balsam send.
To crop the plant the wicked goat presumes,
Whose fetid beard the precious balm perfumes
But in revenge of the unhallow'd theft
The Caitiff's of his larded beard bereft,
Baldness thou dost redress, nor are we sure
Whether the beard or balsam gives the cure.

ABRAHAM COWLEY (1618-67)

CLEMATIS

Mental beauty

T is customary as we part
A trinket — to confer —
It helps to stimulate the faith
— When lovers be afar —

'Tis various — as the various taste —
Clematis — journeying far —
Presents me with a single Curl
Of her Electric Hair —

EMILY DICKINSON (1830-86)

First and chief among such climbers comes the clematis. The name originally meant merely a branch of a vine, but afterwards was extended as a name for almost all climbing plants. Pliny included several such under the name; Gerard says that clematis is "a certain genericke name to all woody winding plants, having certaine affinitie because of the spreading branching and semblance of the vine"; and Parkinson has a chapter headed, "Clematis, Clamberers and Creepers," and the chapter begins with the periwinkle and ends with the passion-flower. Of the true clematis we have one beautiful representative in the traveller's joy (*C. vitalba*), "decking and adorning waies and hedges, where people travel, and thereupon I have named it traveller's joy," says Gerard; and his name has clung to it, though it has not supplanted the older name of "ladies' bower," or "virgin's bower," the last name having been given to it in honour of Queen Elizabeth.

FROM *IN A GLOUCESTERSHIRE GARDEN* BY CANON ELLACOMBE (1822-1916)

LILY-OF-THE-VALLEY

Return of happiness

And the naiad-like lily of the vale,
Whom youth makes so fair and passion so pale,
That the light of its tremulous bells is seen
Through their pavilions of tender green...

FROM *THE SENSITIVE PLANT* BY PERCY BYSSHE SHELLEY

(1792-1822)

C R O C U S
C R O C U S

———

Abuse not

Say, what impels, amidst surrounding snow
Congeal'd, the crocus' flamy bud to glow?
Say, what retards, amidst the summer's blaze,
Th' autumnal bulb, till pale, declining days?

The God of Seasons; whose pervading power
Controls the sun, or sheds the fleecy shower:
He bids each flower His quickening word obey,
Or to each lingering bloom enjoins delay.

FROM *THE NATURAL HISTORY OF SELBORNE* BY GILBERT WHITE (1720-93)

Cyclamen
CYCLAMEN

Diffidence

They are terribly white:
There is snow on the ground,
And a moon on the snow at night;
The sky is cut by the winter light;
Yet I, who have all these things in ken,
Am struck to the heart by the chiselled white
Of this handful of cyclamen.

KATHARINE BRADLEY (1846-1914) AND

EDITH COOPER (1862-1913)

DIANTHUS
PINK

Boldness

Woodley stood among fields; and there was an old-fashioned garden where roses and currant-bushes touched each other, and where the heathery asparagus formed a pretty background to the pinks and gilly-flowers; there was no drive up to the door. We got out at a little gate, and walked up a straight box-edged path.

"My cousin might make a drive, I think," said Miss Pole, who was afraid of ear-ache, and had only her cap on.

"I think it is very pretty," said Miss Matty, with a soft plaintiveness in her voice.

FROM *CRANFORD* BY ELIZABETH GASKELL (1810-65)

DIANTHUS BARBATUS
SWEET WILLIAM

Gallantry

Soon will the high Midsummer pomps come on,
Soon will the musk carnations break and swell,
Soon will we have gold-dusted snapdragon,
Sweet-William with his homely cottage smell,
And stocks in fragrant blow.

FROM *THYRSIS* BY MATTHEW ARNOLD (1822-88)

GALANTHUS

SNOWDROP

Hope

The Snowdrop is the prophet of the flowers;

It lives and dies upon its bed of snows;

And like a thought of spring it comes and goes.

Hanging its head beside our leafless bowers.

The sun's betrothing kiss it never knows,

Nor all the glowing joy of golden showers;

But ever in a placid, pure repose,

More like a spirit with its look serene,

Droops its pale cheek veined thro' with infant green.

FROM *THE WILD ROSE AND THE SNOWDROP* BY

GEORGE MEREDITH (1828-1909)

GERANIUM
CRANESBILL

Steadfast piety

Beautiful Evelyn Hope is dead!
  Sit and watch by her side an hour.
That is her book-shelf, this her bed;
She plucked that piece of geranium-flower,
Beginning to die too, in the glass;
Little has yet been changed, I think:
The shutters are shut, no light may pass
Save two long rays thro' the hinge's chink.

But the time will come, — at last it will,
When, Evelyn Hope, what meant (I shall say)
In the lower earth, in the years long still,
That body and soul so pure and gay?
Why your hair was amber, I shall divine,
And your mouth of your own geranium's red —
And what you would do with me, in fine,
In the new life come in the old one's stead.

ROBERT BROWNING (1812-89)

HEDERA
IVY

Fidelity, Marriage

Round the old walls observe the ivy twine,

A plant attached to grandeur in decline.

The tottering pile she grasps in her embrace,

With a green mask conceals its furrowed face,

And keeps it standing on its time-worn base.

Learn hence, O man! to act the ivy's part,

Fix deep the bright exemplar in thine heart;

To friendship's sacred call with joy attend —

Cling like the ivy, round a falling friend!

Who, when she can no longer prop the wall,

Hugs her old friend, and both together fall.

FROM *CHEPSTOW: A POEM* BY EDWARD DAVIES

(1718-89)

HELIANTHUS
SUNFLOWER

———

Haughtiness

Stately stand the sunflowers, glowing down the garden-side,
Ranged in royal rank arow along the warm grey wall,
Whence their deep disks burn at rich midnoon afire with pride,
Even as though their beams indeed were sunbeams, and the tall
Sceptral stems bore stars whose reign endures, not flowers that fall.
Lowlier laughs and basks the kindlier flower of homelier fame,
Held by love the sweeter that it blooms in Shakespeare's name,
Fragrant yet as though his hand had touched and made it thrill,
Like the whole world's heart, with warm new life and gladdening flame.
Fair befall the fairgreen close that lies below the mill!

FROM *THE MILL GARDEN* BY ALGERNON SWINBURNE (1837-1909)

HYACINTHOIDES
BLUEBELL

———

Constancy

Sacred watcher, wave thy bells!
Fair hill flower and woodland Child!
Dear to me in deep green dells —
Dearest on the mountains wild —
Bluebell, even as all divine

I have seen my darling shine —
Bluebell, even as wan and frail
I have seen my darling ail —
Thou hast found a voice for me —
As soothing words are breathed by thee.

EMILY BRONTË (1818-48)

IRIS
IRIS

Message

T hou art the iris, fair among the fairest,
  Who, armed with golden rod
And winged with the celestial azure, bearest
The message of some God.

Thou art the Muse, who far from crowded cities,
Hauntest the sylvan streams,
Playing on pipes of reed the artless ditties
That come to us as dreams.

FROM *FLOWER-DE-LUCE* BY HENRY WADSWORTH

LONGFELLOW (1807-82)

Jasminum

JASMINE

Amiability

Althea with the purple eye; the broom,
Yellow and bright as bullion unalloyed
Her blossoms; and luxuriant above all
The jasmine, throwing wide her elegant sweets,
The deep dark green of whose unvarnished leaf
Makes more conspicuous, and illumines more
The bright profusion of her scattered stars.

FROM *THE TASK* BY WILLIAM COWPER (1731-1800)

LATHYRUS ODORATUS
SWEET PEA

Delicate pleasures

H ere are sweet peas, on tip-toe for a flight:
With wings of gentle flush o'er delicate white,
And taper finger catching at all things,
To bind them all about with tiny rings.

FROM *I STOOD TIP-TOE UPON A LITTLE HILL* BY JOHN KEATS

(1795-1821)

WHITE LILY

Purity, Sweetness

There is not a flower in the garden again that groweth taller than the Lillie, reaching otherwhile to the height of three cubits from the ground: but a weak and slender neck it hath, and carries it not streight and upright, but it bendeth and noddeth downeward, as being not of strength sufficient to beare the weight of the head standing upon it. The flower is of incomparable whiteness, devided into leaves, without-forth are chamfered, narrow at the bottome, and by little and little spreading broader toward the top: fashioned all together in manner of a broad mouthed cup or beaker, the brims and lips whereof turne up somewhat backward round about and lie very open. Within these leaves there appeare certaine fine threads in manner of seeds: and just in the middest stand yellow chives, like as in Saffron.

FROM *THE NATURAL HISTORY* BY PLINY, TRANSLATED BY PHILEMON HOLLAND (1601)

LILIUM

FIELD LILY

Humility

D own in a meadow fresh and gay,
Picking lillies all the day;
Picking lillies both red and blue,
I little thought what love could do.

Where love is planted there it grows,
It buds and blossoms like any rose,
It has so sweet and a pleasant smell,
No flowers on earth can it excel.

TRADITIONAL RHYME

LONICERA

HONEYSUCKLE

Generous and devoted affection

Fair flower, that dost so comely grow,
Hid in this silent, dull retreat,
Untouched thy honied blossoms blow,
Unseen thy little branches greet.
No roving foot shall crush thee here,
No busy hand provoke a tear.

FROM *THE WILD HONEY SUCKLE* BY PHILIP FRENEAU

(1752-1832)

MAGNOLIA
MAGNOLIA

Love of nature

In the enclosure the spring flowers are almost too beautiful – a great stretch of foam-like cowslips. As I bend over them, the air is heavy and sweet with their scent, like hay and new milk and the kisses of children, and, further on, a sunlit wonder of chiming daffodils.

Before me two great rhododendron bushes. Against the dark, broad leaves the blossoms rise, flame-like, tremulous in the still air, and the pear rose loving-cup of a magnolia hangs delicately on the grey bough.

FROM *In the Botanical Garden* BY KATHERINE

MANSFIELD (1888-1923)

MYOSOTIS

FORGET-ME-NOT

True love

When to the flowers so beautiful,
    The Father gave a name,
Back came a little blue-eyed one,
All timidly it came,
And standing at its Father's feet,
And gazing in His face,
It said in low and trembling tones,
"Dear God the name Thou gavest me
Alas! I have forgot."
Kindly the Father looked Him down,
And said, "Forget-me-not."

ANON.

From off her glowing cheek, she sate and stretched
The silk upon the frame, and worked her name
Between the Moss-rose and Forget-me-not—
Her own dear name, with her own auburn hair!
That forced to wander till sweet spring return,
I yet might ne'er forget her smile, her look,
Her voice (that even in her mirthful mood
Has made me wish to steal away and weep).
Nor yet the entrancement of that maiden kiss
With which she promised, that when spring returned,
She would resign one half of that dear name
And own thenceforth no other name but mine!

THE KEEP-SAKE BY SAMUEL TAYLOR COLERIDGE (1772-1834)

Narcissus
DAFFODIL

Regard

I never saw daffodils so beautiful; they grew among the mossy stones about and about them, some rested their heads upon these stones as on a pillow for weariness and the rest tossed and reeled and danced and seemed as if they verily laughed with the wind that blew upon them over the lake, they looked so gay ever glancing ever changing. This wind blew directly over the lake to them. There was here and there a little knot and a few stragglers a few yards higher up but they were so few as not to disturb the simplicity and unity and life of that one busy highway.

FROM THE JOURNALS OF DOROTHY WORDSWORTH (1771-1855)

Fair daffodils, we weep to see

You haste away so soon:

As yet the early-rising sun

Has not attained his noon.

Stay, stay

Until the hasting day

Has run

But to the evensong;

And, having pray'd together, we

Will go with you along.

We have short time to stay, as you

We have as short a Spring;

As quick a growth to meet decay;

As you, or anything.

We die

As your hours do, and dry

Away

Like to the summer's rain;

Or as the pearls of morning's dew

Ne'er to be found again.

To Daffodils by Robert Herrick

(1591-1674)

ORCHIS
ORCHID

A belle

If nature ever showed her playfulness in the formation of plants, this is visible in the most striking way among orchids...[their flowers] take the form of little birds, of lizards, of insects. They look like a man, a woman, sometimes like an austere, sinister fighter, sometimes like a clown who excites our laughter. They represent the image of a lazy tortoise, a melancholy toad, an agile, ever chattering monkey. Nature has formed orchid flowers in such a way that unless they make us laugh, they surely excite our greatest admiration. The causes of their marvellous variety are (at least in my opinion) hidden by nature under a sacred veil.

FROM *Exoticarum Plantarum Centuria Prima* (1678)

BY JACOB BREYNE

According to Greek mythology the orchid was created from the blood of a satyr's son. The wild youth had violated one of the priestesses at a feast of Bacchus and the furious Bacchanals slew him. When his father complained, the gods made the flower grow from his blood. The orchid was believed to be the food of satyrs, the goat-like deities of the woods, and to be responsible for their dissolute ways. In fact the bulb is high in nutritional content. During the eighteenth century a dish known as salop, made from orchid bulbs, was widely served in the fashionable coffee houses of London.

PAEONIA
PEONY

Shame, Bashfulness

Vulgarity is the idea which had long been associated with the effects of the Paeonia…But there is a race of Paeonias now in cultivation which, for perfection of form and delicacy of colouring, vie with the queen of flowers herself, and many of them are sweet-scented. They embrace all the delicacy of colouring which lies between the pure white, the pale pink, the delicate blush, the brilliant rosy-purple, the crimson, and various other effective and pleasing colours…the flowers are as double and compact as the finest rose, and the blooms of great size.

FROM *THE GARDEN MAGAZINE*, 1874

P eony. According to fable, so called from Paeon, the physician who cured the wounds received by the gods in the Trojan war. The seeds were, at one time, worn round the neck as a charm against the powers of darkness.

> About an Infant's neck hang Paeonie,
>
> It cures Alcydes cruell maladie.

FROM BREWER'S DICTIONARY OF PHRASE AND FABLE, 1870

I t was once widely held that a peony plant will last a lifetime provided it is left undisturbed, while uprooting it will bring bad luck. Anyone wishing to remove a peony had therefore to get a dog to dig it up for them in the dead of night.

PAPAVER
SCARLET POPPY

Fantastic extravagance

In Flanders fields the poppies blow
Between the crosses, row on row,
That mark our place; and in the sky
The larks, still bravely singing, fly
Scarce heard amid the guns below.

We are the Dead. Short days ago
We lived, felt dawn, saw sunset glow,
Loved and were loved, and now we lie
In Flanders fields.

Take up our quarrel with the foe:
To you from failing hands we throw
The torch; be yours to hold it high.
If ye break faith with us who die
We shall not sleep, though poppies grow
In Flanders fields.

JOHN McCrae (1872-1918)

Papaver

WHITE POPPY

———

Sleep, My bane, My antidote

Little brown seed, oh! little brown brother,
What kind of flower will you be?
I'll be a poppy – all white, like my mother;
Do be a poppy, like me.

What! you're a sunflower? How I shall miss you
When you're grown golden and high!
But I shall send all the bees up to kiss you;
Little brown brother, good-bye.

ANON.

· · 49

PASSIFLORA

PASSION FLOWER

Religious superstition

When the first European travellers in Brazil found the passion flower growing, they identifed almost every aspect of it with Christ's Passion. In the leaves they saw the spear that pierced His side; in the five anthers His five wounds; in the tendrils the whip that scourged Him; in the central column the upright of the Cross; in the three styles the three nails; and in the threads within the flowers the crown of thorns. Later missionaries believed that the luxuriant growth and the many flowers of the plant represented the conversion of the native peoples to Christianity.

PRIMULA VULGARIS

PRIMROSE

Early youth

Help us to tell her tales of years gone by,
   And this sweet spring, the best beloved and best;
Joy will be flown in its mortality;
Something must stay to tell us of the rest.
Here, thronged with primroses, the steep rock's breast
Glittered at evening like a starry sky;
And in this bush our sparrow built her nest,
Of which I sang one song that will not die.

FROM *A FAREWELL* BY WILLIAM WORDSWORTH (1770-1850)

Ranunculus
Buttercup

———

Ingratitude, Childishness

The flush of life may well be seen
Thrilling back over hills and valleys;
The cowslip startles its meadows`green,
The buttercup catches the sun in its chalice
And there's never a leaf or a blade too mean
To be some happy creature's palace.

from *What Is So Rare as a Day in June?* by

James Russell Lowell (1819-91)

Rosa

ROSE

Thy smile I aspire to

O riginally, no doubt, when this pretty custom was first instituted, it may have had a sincere and modest import. Each youth and damsel, gathering bouquets of field-flowers, or the sweetest and fairest that grew in their own gardens, all fresh and virgin blossoms, flung them, with true aim, at the one, or few, whom they regarded with a sentiment of shy partiality at least, if not with love. Often, the lover in the Corso may thus have received from his bright mistress, in her father's princely balcony, the first sweet intimation that his passionate glances had not struck against a heart of marble. What more appropriate mode of suggesting her tender secret could a maiden find than by the soft hit of a rosebud against a young man's cheek.

FROM *THE MARBLE FAUN* BY NATHANIEL HAWTHORNE (1804-64)

Rosa eglanteria
SWEET BRIAR

I wound to heal

I know a bank whereon the wild thyme blows,
Where oxlips and the nodding violet grows
Quite over-canopied with lush woodbine,
With sweet musk-roses, and with eglantine:
There sleeps Titania sometime of the night,
Lull'd in these flowers with dances and delight…

FROM *A Midsummer Night's Dream* BY
WILLIAM SHAKESPEARE (1564-1616)

SCABIOSA
SCABIOUS

Unfortunate love

My borders they should lie a little flue
And rear the finest flowers that sip the dew
The roses blush the lilies vying snow
Should uniform their namles beauties show,

With fine ranuncullus and jonquil fair
That sweet perfumer of the evening air
The scabious too so jocolately dusk
Should there be seen with tufts of smelling musk.

FROM *THE WISH* BY JOHN CLARE (1793-1864)

SOLIDAGO
GOLDEN ROD

Precaution

There were also whole fields full of ferns, now rusty and withering, which in older countries are commonly confined to wet ground. There were very few flowers, even allowing for the lateness of the season. It chanced that I saw no asters in bloom along the road for fifty miles, though they were so abundant then in Massachusetts…and no golden-rods till within twenty miles of Monson, where I saw a three-ribbed one.

FROM *THE MAINE WOODS* BY HENRY DAVID THOREAU (1817-62)

SYRINGA
LILAC

Humility

I n the dooryard fronting an old farm-house near the white-wash'd palings,

Stands the lilac-bush tall-growing with heart-shaped leaves of rich green,

With many a pointed blossom rising delicate, with the perfume strong I love,

With every leaf a miracle – and from this bush in the dooryard,

With delicate-color'd blossoms and heart-shaped leaves of rich green,

A sprig with its flower I break.

FROM *MEMORIES OF PRESIDENT LINCOLN* BY WALT WHITMAN (1819-92)

VARIEGATED TULIP

———

Beautiful eyes

Then comes the tulip race, where beauty plays

Her idle freaks; from family diffused

To family, as flies the father-dust,

The varied colours run; and, while they break

On the charmed eye th' exulting florist marks,

With secret pride, the wonders of his hand.

FROM *THE SEASONS* BY JAMES THOMSON (1700-48)

TULIPA

TULIP

Fame

Spring boxes for the veranda steps have been filled with pink and white and yellow tulips. I love tulips better than any other spring flower; they are the embodiment of alert cheerfulness and tidy grace, and next to a hyacinth look like a wholesome, freshly tubbed young girl beside a stout lady whose every movement weighs down the air with patchouli. Their faint, delicate scent is refinement itself; and is there anything in the world more charming than the sprightly way they hold up their little faces to the sun? I have heard them called bold and flaunting, but to me they seem modest grace itself, only always on the alert to enjoy life as much as they can and not afraid of looking the sun or anything else above them in the face. On the grass there are two beds of them carpeted with forget-me-nots.

FROM *ELIZABETH AND HER GERMAN GARDEN* BY COUNTESS VON ARNIM (1866-1941)

VIOLA

VIOLET

Watchfulness

Roses, damask and red, are fast flowers of their smells; so that you may walk by a whole row of them, and find nothing of their sweetness; yea, though it be in a morning's dew. Bays, likewise, yield no smell, as they grow, rosemary little, nor sweet marjoram; that which, above all others, yields the sweetest smell in the air, is the violet, especially the white double violet, which comes twice a year, about the middle of April, and about Bartholomew-tide.

OF GARDENS, ESSAYS, FRANCIS BACON

(1561-1626)

VINCA
WHITE PERIWINKLE

Pleasures of memory

MARCH 10

When I got to the bottom of the lane, I set my bicycle against a bank and picniced [sic] on a fence. A beautiful Jay in all the glory of his spring plumage flew screaming across the lane into a spinney of larch trees opposite. He seemed to resent the intrusion of a human being in such an unfrequented spot. I was glad to find the white Periwinkle still trailing its wreathes on the bank; but the flowers were only in bud; and the Violets too, were just uncurling their buds under their fresh green leaves… I noticed that the white Periwinkle blossoms have five petals, while the blue have only four. I wonder if this is always so.

FROM THE JOURNAL OF EDITH HOLDEN (1871-1920)

A LIST OF FLOWER MEANINGS

ACACIA: *Friendship*

ACACIA, ROSE OR WHITE:
Elegance

ACACIA, YELLOW: *Secret love*

ACANTHUS: *The fine arts. Artifice*

ACONITE (WOLF'S BANE):
Misanthropy

ACONITE, CROWSFOOT: *Lustre*

AFRICAN MARIGOLD: *Vulgar minds*

AGRIMONY: *Thankfulness.*
Gratitude

ALMOND (COMMON): *Stupidity.*
Indiscretion

ALOE: *Grief. Religious*
supersitition

ALYSSUM (SWEET): *Worth beyond*
beauty

AMARYLLIS: *Pride. Timidity.*
Splendid beauty

AMERICAN LINDEN: *Matrimony*

AMETHYST: *Admiration*

ANEMONE (GARDEN): *Forsaken*

ANGELICA: *Inspiration*

APPLE: *Temptation*

APPLE (BLOSSOM): *Preference. Fame*
speaks him great and good

ASPEN TREE: *Lamentation*

ASTER (CHINA): *Variety.*
Afterthought

AURICULA: *Painting*

AZALEA: *Temperance*

BACHELOR'S BUTTONS: *Celibacy*

BASIL: *Hatred*

BAY LEAF: *I change but in death*

BAY TREE: *Glory*

BELLADONNA: *Silence*

BELLFLOWER, PYRAMIDAL:
Constancy

BETONY: *Surprise*

BIRCH: *Meekness*

BLUEBELL: *Constancy*

BORAGE: *Bluntness*

BRAMBLE: *Lowliness. Envy.*
Remorse

BROOM: *Humility. Neatness*

BULRUSH: *Indiscretion. Docility*

BURDOCK: *Importunity. Touch me*
not

BUTTERCUP (KINGCUP):
Ingratitude. Childishness

CACTUS: *Warmth*

CANDYTUFT: *Indifference*

CANTERBURY BELL:
Acknowledgement

CARNATION, DEEP RED: *Alas! for*
my poor heart

CARNATION, STRIPED: *Refusal*

CARNATION, YELLOW: *Disdain*

CEDAR: *Strength*

CEDAR OF LEBANON: *Incorruptible*

CELANDINE (LESSER): *Joys to come*

CHAMOMILE: *Energy in adversity*

CHINA ASTER: *Variety*

CHINA ROSE: *Beauty always new*

CHRISTMAS ROSE: *Relieve my*
anxiety

CHRYSANTHEMUM, RED: *I love*

CHRYSANTHEMUM, WHITE: *Truth*

CHRYSANTHEMUM, YELLOW:
Slighted love

CITRON: *Ill-natured beauty*

CLEMATIS: *Mental beauty*

CLEMATIS, EVERGREEN: *Poverty*

CLOVES: *Dignity*

COLTSFOOT: *Justice shall be done*

COLUMBINE, PURPLE: *Resolved to*
win

COLUMBINE, RED: *Anxious and*
trembling

COREOPSIS: *Always cheerful*

CORIANDER: *Hidden worth*

COWSLIP: *Pensiveness. Winning*
grace

COWSLIP, AMERICAN: *Divine*
beauty. You are my divinity

CRANBERRY: *Cure for heartache*

CROCUS: *Abuse not*

CROCUS, SPRING: *Youthful*
gladness

CROCUS, SAFFRON: *Mirth*

CROWN IMPERIAL: *Majesty. Power*

DAFFODIL: *Regard*

DAHLIA: *Instability*

DAISY: *Innocence*

DAISY, GARDEN: *I share your*
sentiments

DAISY, PARTY-COLOURED: *Beauty*

DAISY, WILD: *I will think of it*

DAMASK ROSE: *Brilliant*
complexion

DANDELION: *Rustic oracle*

DAPHNE ODORA: *Painting the lily*

DOGWOOD: *Durability*

EGLANTINE (SWEET BRIAR): *Poetry. I wound to heal*

FORGET-ME-NOT: *True love. Forget me not*

FOXGLOVE: *Insincerity*

FRENCH HONEYSUCKLE: *Rustic beauty*

FRENCH MARIGOLD: *Jealousy*

GARDEN ANEMONE: *Forsaken*

GERANIUM, DARK: *Melancholy*

GERANIUM, IVY: *Bridal favour*

GERANIUM, ROSE-SCENTED: *Preference*

GILLYFLOWER: *Bonds of affection*

GLORY FLOWER: *Glorious beauty*

GOAT'S RUE: *Reason*

GOLDEN ROD: *Precaution*

GUELDER ROSE: *Winter. Age*

HAREBELL: *Submission. Grief*

HAWTHORN: *Hope*

HOLLY: *Foresight*

HOLLYHOCK: *Ambition. Fecundity*

HONESTY: *Honesty. Fascination*

HONEYSUCKLE: *Generous and devoted affection*

HYACINTH: *Sport. Game. Play*

HYDRANGEA: *A boaster. Heartlessness*

HYSSOP: *Cleanliness*

IRIS: *Message*

IVY: *Fidelity. Marriage*

JACOB'S LADDER: *Come down*

JASMINE: *Amiability*

JUDAS TREE: *Unbelief. Betrayal*

JUNIPER: *Succour. Protection*

LABURNUM: *Forsaken. Pensive beauty*

LADY'S SLIPPER: *Capricious beauty. Win me and wear me*

LARCH: *Audacity. Boldness*

LARKSPUR: *Lightness. Levity*

LAUREL: *Glory*

LAVENDER: *Distrust*

LEMON: *Zest*

LEMON BLOSSOMS: *Fidelity in love*

LILAC, PURPLE: *First love*

LILAC, WHITE: *Youthful Innocence*

LILY, DAY: *Coquetry*

LILY, IMPERIAL: *Majesty*

LILY-OF-THE-VALLEY: *Return of happiness*

LOBELIA: *Malevolence*

LONDON PRIDE: *Frivolity*

LOVE-IN-A-MIST: *Perplexity*

LOVE-LIES-BLEEDING: *Hopeless, not heartless*

MARIGOLD: *Grief*

MARJORAM: *Blushes*

MEADOW SAFFRON: *My best days are past*

MEADOWSWEET: *Uselessness*

MESEMBRYANTHEMUM: *Idleness*

MIMOSA (SENSITIVE PLANT): *Sensitiveness*

MISTLETOE: *I surmount difficulties*

MORNING GLORY: *Affectation*

MOUNTAIN ASH: *Prudence*

NARCISSUS: *Egotism*

NASTURTIUM: *Patriotism*

ORANGE BLOSSOMS: *Your purity equals your loveliness*

OX EYE DAISY: *Patience*

PANSY: *Thoughts*

PEA, EVERLASTING: *An appointed meeting. Lasting Pleasure*

PENNYROYAL: *Flee away*

PERIWINKLE, BLUE: *Early friendship*

PERIWINKLE, WHITE: *Pleasures of memory*

PINK: *Boldness*

POLYANTHUS: *Pride of riches*

POPPY, RED: *Consolation*

POPPY, WHITE: *Sleep. My bane. My antidote*

PRIMROSE: *Early youth*

PRIMROSE, EVENING: *Inconstancy*

RANUNCULUS: *You are radiant with charms*

ROCKET: *Rivalry*

ROSE: *Love*

ROSE, CABBAGE: *Ambassador of love*

ROSE, DOG: *Pleasure and pain*

ROSE, MULTIFLORA: *Grace*

ROSE, MUNDI: *Variety*

ROSE, MUSK: *Capricious beauty*

ROSE, WHITE: *I am worthy of you*

ROSE, YELLOW: *Jealousy*

ROSEBUD, RED: *Pure and lovely*

ROSEBUD, WHITE: *Girlhood*

ROSEBUD, MOSS: *Confession of love*

SNAPDRAGON: *Presumption*

SNOWDROP: *Hope*

STAR OF BETHLEHEM: *Purity*

SUNFLOWER, DWARF: *Adoration*

SUNFLOWER, TALL: *Haughtiness*

SWEET PEA: *Delicate pleasures*

VIOLET, BLUE: *Faithfulness*

WATER LILY: *Purity of heart*

XANTHIUM: *Rudeness. Pertinacity*

ZINNIA: *Thoughts of absent friends*

Picture Acknowledgements

The Publishers would like to thank the picture libraries below for permission to reproduce the following paintings in this book:

E.T. Archive: p43 Manuscript *Wild Daffodil and Red Admiral Butterfly*, Victoria and Albert Museum.

Fine Art Photographic: p2 Eloise Harriet Stannard *A Still Life of Chrysanthemums*, Burlington Paintings; p7 Anthonore Eleanore Christensen *Anemones and Primroses in a Basket*, Eaton Gallery; p9 Maria Dorothea Krabbe *Anemones and Forget-me-nots*, Philip Parker Esq.; p10 Thomas Worsey *Still Life of Foxgloves, Mushrooms, Snapdragons and Thistles*, Antony Mitchell Fine Paintings; p12 Berthe de la Baume *A Still Life of Asters, Pears and Apples*, Colin Stodgell; p13 Andrew Nicholl *The Flowers of the Field*; p16 Harald Martin Hansen Holm *Chrysanthemums*, Cambridge Fine Art; p18 Basil Besler *Clematis Coerulea Pannonica*, Trowbridge Gallery; p19 Emile Faivre *A Still Life of Clematis*; p23 Oluf August Hermansen *A Peony, Pinks and an Anemone*; p24 Annie M. Youngman *A Still Life of Pinks*, Private Collection; p25 Leo Louppe *Still Life of Carnations*, Mark Hancock; p26 Johan Laurentz Jensen *Rubrum Lilies and Fuchsias*, Verner Amell Limited; p27 John Atkinson Grimshaw *Fair Maids of February*; p28 Robert Bateman *Wild Geranium and Great Masterwort*; p31 Daniel Sherrin *The Bluebell Walk*, Private Collection; p32 Alfred Godchaux *A Still Life of Iris and Roses*, Gavin Graham; p36 Walter Crane *The Garden*; p41 Mary Elizabeth Duffield *Spring Flowers – Forget-me-not*; p46 Madeleine Lemaire *Peonies and Roses*, Baumkotter Gallery; p49 Anonymous *A Poppy Basket*, Private Collection; p50 Christine Lovmand *A Still Life of a Cactus, Lilies and Passion Flowers on a Windowsill*; p57 Eugene Henri Cauchois *Springtime*, Stodgell Gallery; p58 Philippe Rousseau *A Rich Still Life of Tulips by an Urn*. Front Jacket: Annie Feray Mutrie *Spring Flowers*; Back Jacket Walter John James *Still Life of Flowers*; Back Flap: Pauline Caspers *A Rich Still Life of Lilac and Peonies*.

Visual Arts Library: p8 Thomas Sychkou *Beside the Hollyhocks*; p20 Emma Loffler *Blossom and Lily-of-the-Valley*; p21 Johan Laurentz Jensen *Crocus on a Table*; p30 Paul Gauguin *The Sunflowers*, Musée de l'Ermitage; p33 John Jessop Hardwick *Iris and Christmas Rose*, Chris Beetles Gallery; p39 George Dionysius Ehret *Magnolia*; p48 Augusta Laessoe *Wild Roses, Poppies and Marguerites*; p51 Lais Hansen *Primroses and Other Flowers*; p53 Johan Laurentz Jensen *A Bouquet of Roses*; p59 J. B. Dry *Corner of Mr. de la Bruyère's Garden*, Detroit Institute of Art.